Waiting on the Lord
30 Reflections

Barbara Hartzler

MORE TITLES BY BARBARA HARTZLER

<u>The Nexis Series:</u>

The Nexis Secret

Crossing Nexis (2016)

The Nexis Conspiracy (2016)

The Nexis Crusade (2016)

Waiting on the Lord
30 Reflections

Barbara Hartzler

First Printing, 2015

Blue Herbie Press
www.barbarahartzler.com

ISBN: 0692463534
ISBN-13: 978-0-692-46353-6

To Sam for being the perfect person to wait with

CONTENTS

INTRODUCTION

If you're reading this devotional, then you're probably in a time of waiting on the Lord like I've been for the last several years. This thirty-day devotional comes from a time of personal anguish and soul-searching that has been one of the hardest times of my life. Yet, it's also been the most rewarding journey I've ever taken.

Why was I waiting on the Lord? In several areas in my life I felt God telling me to wait on him for deliverance, personal healing, and freedom from infertility. In other areas of my life the waiting was forced on me. Suddenly my publishing contract didn't look so good. Then we started facing financial difficulties related to the work injury I'd been waiting on the Lord to heal. When I realized God was telling me to wait, at first it made me angry. That's all the direction I received for a long period of time. But my anger led to a desperation for the Lord where he ultimately helped me learn the most valuable lessons of all—trust, faith, surrender, and dependence on God.

Because of my time waiting on the Lord, I finally feel like I'm getting closer to the woman of God I was always meant to become. The trials I persevered through honed and shaped my character and my dependence on God.

It was a hard lesson for me to learn, because I do not come from a Christian family. Indeed, my childhood was littered with dramatic upheaval and times where we were not safe in our own home. After my parents divorced at age four because of drug and alcohol problems, my mother married a man with mental health issues. When he didn't take his medicine he got angry. Not violent enough to ever hit us, but after a few holes in the wall we didn't stick around to test that theory. Instead, we'd stay at his parents' house and wait out the storm. After seven years, they divorced and my father started living with a woman with mental health issues. Our normal visits to Dad's house every other weekend became more and more sporadic.

In middle school, I met some great new friends, one of whom invited us to church. Her mother drove us all to youth group in her little hatchback. When I was fourteen, I found Jesus and gave my life over to him. At seventeen I went to Bible college to learn all I could about my new faith. During college, my sister who had been coming to church with me slipped into the drug scene. She wouldn't get sober for another fourteen years.

Yet through all of that, God was always with me, protecting me and guiding me to the next step. A few years after college I married a wonderful man who shared my faith. I started working on my first novel and joined a writers group. Then I got laid off and had to take a job at an online university. It eventually turned into a data entry position, and I started feeling horrible pain in my hands, and then my elbows. They labeled it tendonitis and epicondylitis, precursors to carpal tunnel syndrome. My writing got put on hold. The pain was so horrible it kept me up at night. Often, I had to sleep on the couch and couldn't fall asleep until four in the morning. After about a year and a half of taking leave and seeing doctors, I finally got fired. Pain-wise, it was a relief. Money-wise, we were in trouble.

I couldn't work for another eighteen months while I recovered from the injury. During that time we had no idea where the money we needed to survive was going to come from. My former job disputed my unemployment. Then the worker's compensation legal process took much longer than we expected.

Needless to say, I was desperate for God. My husband was very supportive, but it hurt him deeply to see me in so much pain. No one could help us, apart from God. He sustained me through the most excruciating parts of my suffering, but it was a hard journey. At times both my husband and I were angry. We blamed God, until we realized that he was the only one who could get us through the suffering.

And he kept coming through for us. During those eighteen months of my recovery, he gave us victory in unemployment appeals court, and six months later a settlement from our worker's compensation claim. We didn't know what would happen, but there's no way we could've made it eighteen months on one income without God's help.

During my recovery I finally decided I couldn't start the day without seeking God. I needed him that much. I spent an hour or two every morning praying, reading four or five devotionals, and worshiping God. And he met me at my point of need. He led me to some great verses and great Bible resources to help me see just how much I needed him. I learned to trust him, broke free from the sin issues I'd struggled with for years, and even laid the anger down at his feet. I learned to let go and trust God, even when I had no idea what the outcome would be. But believing God is who he says he is, and he'll do what he says he will do, is enough for me. Because he truly is all I need.

For so long I struggled with every emotion that comes with waiting on the Lord. Many times I felt like I deserved the pain, like it was some kind of punishment because I was far from perfect. But through God's word I recognized what a nasty lie from the enemy that really was. All of the devotionals in this little book come from something I used to believe that turned out to be a lie. I don't want anyone else in this life to have to learn the hard way like I did. You can be set free from anything, including the lies of the enemy that invade your mind. My prayer is that you let God's truth reveal all the lies you've been believing. Only he can turn all of this around for good. Let today be the day you start letting him work in your heart.

As you wait on the Lord, may he come through for you in such a powerful way that you'll never let go of him.

Blessings to you, my fellow traveler on God's great journey,

Barbara Hartzler

DAY 1

Psalm 68:19

"Praise be to the Lord, to God our Savior, who daily bears our burdens."

Since we're at the beginning of our "Waiting on the Lord" journey, let's start with first things first. If the Lord's been telling you to wait on something big—like healing, finances, or job situations—then you know how hard it is to wait. Especially for an impatient person like me. That's why I stopped praying for patience long ago, because God seems to already have that lesson laid out for me.

What's the first thing that happens when we're told to wait? I know what my default is—I start looking for something to do while I'm waiting. Then I try to find other solutions. Apart from God. It's easy to lose focus and get sidetracked. After all, we're supposed to be self-sufficient, able to fend for ourselves, and figure things out on our own. For me, there's also a stubborn streak to stick to the solutions I painstakingly came up with. That's why this is my life verse. Because I need it. Correction, I REALLY need to remind myself that I'm not in control. Because God's the one who bears my burdens. And he will bear yours, too. You just have to let go and let him take the load.

Easier in theory than in practice, right? Maybe it seems like you're the maker of your current predicament, or maybe you have no idea how you ended up in the waiting room of life right now. Either way, it doesn't matter. You're here, in a place of waiting. In reality, that means you're waiting on God to move, to provide, to give you new direction. Even though it's a scary time of life, waiting also comes with its own blessings, some of which we'll touch on in the next thirty days. It's in the waiting that God has a chance to speak to you like never before. Please don't miss out on what God has for you. Even in a tough time like this.

So here's what I want you to do. I want you to stop for a moment, take a breath, and remember who is really in charge.

God holds the universe in his hands, and he holds your personal world, too. He knows exactly what you're dealing with right now and he's not going to let you walk away empty-handed. No loving father would. He wants to carry your burdens today.

Take time right now to press into his presence. Because all he wants to do is draw you closer to him. He wants you to know him more. He wants to use times like this to speak over your uncertainty, your fear, and your doubt. You can be completely honest with him and bring it all to him. All the hurt, pain, and anger you want to hurl at him. He can handle it. Madeleine L'Engle words this truth with simplicity in her book, *A Ring of Endless Light*. "God can handle your anger."

It's okay to be honest with God, because he can handle your frustration. Just read through the Psalms and you'll see great men of the Bible pouring out their hearts to God. Even their anger and frustration. But they always ended up praising God, surrendering to him, or praying to him for help. The Psalmists paved the way for us to have the freedom to do the same. So be open with the Lord, then let him take care of it for you. You don't have to hold onto your burdens any more.

Lord, you know everything I'm feeling. All the anger and frustration I can't seem to let go of. But here I am waiting, and I know you are here, too. I don't want to rush onward without you and miss out on your blessings that only come through waiting. Instead, I choose to pause and rest in your arms—until you move me forward. Pour your love out over my frustrations and bear my burdens today, I pray. Amen.

Bonus: Read the rest of my favorite verses in this Psalm 68:20, 28, & 32-35.

DAY 2

Proverbs 29:11

"A fool gives full vent to his anger, but a wise man keeps himself under control."

In yesterday's devotion I wrote about God being able to handle your anger. Don't worry, that's still true. But there's a difference between letting God handle your anger, and letting your anger separate you from God. It's a place everyone tends to go naturally at some point, but it's important to remember the difference. The key is to let go of that anger and give it over to him so he can carry the burden. If we hold onto anger too tightly, we end up building a wall between ourselves and God. When that happens the enemy wins. His goal is to distract us from God's truth and put distance between us and God. That's why the waiting stage is such a critical time. Not only is it a place where God can bless us more than we ever imagined, but if we're not careful, it's often a spot where the enemy gains a foothold.

You've heard all kinds of stories where people blame God for letting bad things happen. Unfortunately, I must admit that's my first instinct, too. Back when I tried to do everything on my own, I'd bottle up all of those hurt feelings. Then they'd just be trapped. Festering. With nowhere to go. Even though I didn't want to let my anger come between me and God, deep down it was still bottled up. Instead of a wall, it felt like I'd built a trench between me and God. It's only when I started to figure out how much I needed to let my anger go, that I started to finally believe God could really handle my anger.

I'm not saying I'm perfect and I always let only God have all of my anger and never let it separate us. Because using words like always and never is almost never entirely accurate. Sometimes, my frustration leeches out on other people, or I hold onto it too long and distance myself from God again. Hey, I'm just like you—human. I still have to come back to this principle time and time again. Because not only am I imperfect, but we live in an imperfect world. Things are messed up, and once you think you've got it handled, another mess pops up. That's why God gave us his Word, and each other. He knows how much we need him, and he wants us to turn to him first. So, I challenge you to try this principle right now, or the next time you're angry. Turn to God first, let him have all of your anger, but also surrender that anger to him to deal with as only he can.

Lord, only you know how far-reaching this anger inside of me is. That's why I'm here today, to let it go and let the healing process begin. I want to let it go, but I don't know how. So take this anger, frustration, and hurt boiling up inside me. I surrender it to you. Please bear this burden for me, and deliver me from bitterness as only you can. Let me feel your arms around me, your Holy Spirit ministering to me. Fill me with comfort and a peace that passes all understanding today, I pray. Amen.

Bonus: Read Proverbs 29:6, 8, 25 and Ephesians 4:25-5:2.

DAY 3

Isaiah 41:9-10

"I took you from the ends of the earth, from its farthest corners I called you. I said, 'You are my servant'; I have chosen you and have not rejected you. So do not fear, for I am with you; do not be dismayed, for I am your God. I will strengthen you and help you; I will uphold you with my righteous right hand."

These verses from Isaiah tell us exactly what God really thinks of us. Not the lies we tell ourselves—things like, we're not good enough, or we're going through this awful trial because he's punishing us. If we're trying to live for God, that is far from the truth. He chose every one of us to be here on this planet and walk the earth for the number of days he has for us. If we're chosen by God it means he's not rejecting us. In fact, God never rejects anyone who cries out to him. We're his children and he loves each of us dearly.

No matter where your journey has taken you, God is calling you—right where you are. There's no "far corner" that God can't reach, because he is always with you. He wants you to know him better and feel his presence right alongside you. In his presence there's overwhelming peace, enough to cast aside your fear and give you the hope you need to conquer dismay.

Do you feel God calling you to something specific? Pray about it and let this verse speak to you. For me this verse is all about my call to write, but for you it may mean something completely different. If you're not sure what God's calling you to do, ask him to speak to you today.

He wants to "strengthen you and help you" every step of the way. Even when you come up against opposition and people "rage against you" as verse 11 says. God will take care of anything that comes against you, and if you're still wondering just read verse 12. "Though you search for your enemies, you will not find them. Those who wage war against you will be as nothing at all."

Don't you just love how God promises to take care of you? This is the very reason why I leave finding justice up to God alone. He is the true judge and jury, he knows who our real enemies are. And he knows how to take care of them.

I know this is difficult and maybe even scary. But God will strengthen, help, and uphold you with his righteous hand. Step out in faith. Let go of your fear and dismay. If you do, I guarantee you won't regret serving God. He will speak to you and bless you for being obedient to his call.

Lord, thank you for this reminder that you've called me and chosen me. That I am not rejected by you in any way. Help me to feel that truth in my heart. Speak to me about your calling. Show me that you're with me right now. Today I'm letting go of the fear and dismay I've carried for so long. Please strengthen me and help me. Uphold me with your righteous right hand. Amen.

Bonus: Read Isaiah 41:8-14.

DAY 4

Exodus 14:14

"The Lord will fight for you; you need only to be still."

I love this verse because it's a great reminder of something we're sorely lacking in modern society. Stillness. In today's culture it's all about running and rushing, going and doing. While there's nothing wrong with these things, there is also a place for stillness. Sometimes it's necessary to pause and contemplate.

Are you struggling with waiting? I know I did. Stop for a minute. Breathe in the Lord's presence. Evaluate your priorities.

I found Jesus when I was fourteen and a friend invited me to church. I didn't grow up in a Christian home and it was something I thought I had to overcome to find a place in God's kingdom. I tried so hard to be the perfect Christian. I even went to Bible college and worked at a church after I graduated. But it wasn't enough. I never felt good enough.

So when God dropped me in the waiting zone, I rebelled. I got angry and railed at him. I blamed him for keeping me so frustratingly stuck. But being mad at God and trying to do this all on my own only left me exhausted. All my inspiration dried up until I couldn't do anything except the one thing I didn't want to do—change my priorities.

When I started putting God first, that's when I finally saw his hand working in my life. And I don't just mean that I stopped rebelling. I actually set aside an hour or two in the morning to seek God and wait on him. By doing the opposite of what I felt, I was finally able to surrender my own stubborn will to God. That's when I saw how much he really was fighting for me—when I at last came to a place of stillness.

God's combat mission for me wasn't on the front I thought it was. Instead of battling the cause of my pain and suffering, God was actually fighting on the home front of my heart. He didn't want to change my circumstances. He wanted to change my heart. While I would never wish that much pain on anyone, I know that what the enemy intended to derail me is what God ended up using to get me back on track. But I did have a role in changing my heart as well. My job was to stop fighting God and surrender to him. He fights our battles for us and triumphs in ways we could never think of or imagine. We need only to be still.

Lord you know my heart, you know exactly what I'm dealing with. It comes as no surprise to you. But it's a surprise to me. I don't know what to do, where to go, or who to turn to in my distress. So right now I turn to you. I lay myself and my circumstances at your feet. Help me stop fighting you. Help me be still so you can fight my battles as only you can. Amen.

Bonus: Read Exodus 14:13 or all of Exodus 14.

Recommended reading: Beth Moore, *Praying God's Word Day by Day* April 2 devotional

DAY 5

"Have mercy on me, O God, according to your unfailing love; according to your great compassion blot out my transgressions. Wash away all my iniquity and cleanse me from my sin. Create in me a pure heart, O God, and renew a steadfast spirit within me. Do not cast me from your presence or take your Holy Spirit from me. Restore to me the joy of your salvation and grant me a willing spirit, to sustain me."

Repentance is the first step toward freedom, wholeness, and a steadfast spirit. In the in-between time where we find ourselves waiting on the Lord, it can make us feel frustrated and stuck, looking for someone to blame. Even if we've released our anger to God, there are times when it's all too easy to point the blame finger at ourselves. Whether it's something we've dug up from the past or something we're struggling with now, the enemy can always point out all the ways we fall short. Because let's face it, we're all imperfect people. That's why we need God. Only he can make things right for us. Only he can wipe the slate clean.

Isn't it time to open yourself up to new life? Even if we feel completely stuck and stagnant with no hope for relief, God wants to refresh us "according to his unfailing love." He wants to "blot out my transgressions" with his mercy. Even more than that, God wants to wash away the past and give us a fresh start. To make us new creatures in him, with pure hearts and steadfast spirits. After the roller-coaster ride of emotions we take while we wait on God, wouldn't it be nice to be steadfast for once?

That steadfast spirit can be ours if we continue to seek his presence. For in God's presence we'll find mercy, unfailing love, and abounding compassion. Not only that, but he'll send his Holy Spirit to restore our joy and give us a willing spirit. Above all else, in God's presence we'll find the sustaining life we need to carry on. We can slog through the dark trenches ahead and press on.

In so many things in life, God's word has more than one meaning. So when he says he wants to renew a steadfast spirit in you it's not just because he wants to build you up right now. He also wants to prepare you for the hard times you'll face in the future. Because it takes a mountain of steadfastness to press on when it seems like there's no end in sight. But there is light up ahead. With God on your side you CAN slog through the darkness and make it through to the other side.

God, it's easy to stumble when all I see is blackness. Lift my gaze today, I pray, and help me see the sliver of light you're shining in the darkness. Right now I repent for all the things I've done in anger and frustration. Jesus, cleanse me from my sin right now, and wash it all away. Even the past failures I've hung above the door of my heart. Instead of dwelling on my failings, Lord I ask you to create a new heart in me. Make my spirit steadfast in the midst of it all. Holy Spirit, restore to me the joy of my salvation. Bless me with a willing spirit, and sustain me from this moment on. In your name I pray, amen.

Bonus: Read all of Psalm 51.

DAY 6

Romans 8:1-2

"Therefore there is now no condemnation for those who are in Christ Jesus, because through Christ Jesus the law of the Spirit of life set me free from the law of sin and death."

After we fess up to our sins and submit by repenting of them before God, there tends to be some lingering condemnation. That's why this is one of my go-to verses. Because no matter how much I believe God is willing and able to forgive my sins through the blood of Jesus, it's still so unbelievable. It's human nature to expect someone to still be angry when you've wronged them, even if they've said, "I forgive you."

God's nature is not the same as man's. His nature is completely divine and completely different than ours. I'm glad for his divine nature that says my sins are forgiven, my failures washed away, and my slate wiped clean. But even more than that, there is no condemnation because, "the Spirit of life set me free from the law of sin and death."

Pause for a moment and let those words sink in. If you've surrendered your sin to Jesus and have let him wash you clean, you are now set free. Set free from what? From condemnation, the law, all guilt, shame, and regret that comes with living by impossible standards. It's true. You're free. But the next question I like to ask is, "Now what?"

What do you think God could be setting you free to do? Once your thoughts aren't plagued by condemnation your mind is free to think on so many other things—joy, peace, hope, and the blessings that God has given you. And God wants to build you up in ways you could never imagine, so you can pour out your newfound joy into other people who are hurting.

Maybe freedom and joy seem hard to believe right now in your present circumstances. I know when I was in the midst of excruciating physical pain and all I wanted was relief, it was really hard to believe I was free from condemnation. Sometimes it felt like I deserved it—like I was being punished. When I was beyond frustrated waiting for God to answer my prayers, it was hard to believe then, too.

Finally, I got to a point where I couldn't rely on ANYTHING else but God. That's when he spoke to my heart. I was free the whole time, but I had been believing lies for far too long. God didn't wait one moment too long. He showed me the next step exactly when I needed to know it.

I wish I could tell you how easy waiting on the Lord is. But I can't. Frankly, it's one of the hardest things I've ever done. The truth is, it's also been the most rewarding time of my life. My faith has been tested and stretched to limits I never knew I had. And God always proved faithful.

I know he'll do the same for you. It's a process. The rewards you'll reap in faith and freedom are infinitely worth the fight. So keep struggling, my friend. And keep seeking God in the midst of your hard times.

Lord, sometimes it's so hard to believe that the struggles I'm facing today could ever lead to something good. But that's why I'm here today, to ask you to help me face my struggles head-on. Speak the truth of these verses into my heart today, and banish any lingering condemnation from my heart and mind. Set me free, I pray, to live the life you've called me to live. Give me hope in the waiting. Pour your joy and peace into my heart right now. In your name I pray, amen.

Bonus: Read Romans chapter 8.

DAY 7

Deuteronomy 31:6

"Be strong and courageous. Do not be afraid or terrified because of them, for the Lord your God goes with you; he will never leave you nor forsake you."

This is one verse that I've written down on a note card and keep handy. I suggest you do the same if it speaks to you. When I'm facing fear, doubt, or any kind of uncertainty, I need this truth to remind myself who's on my side. God doesn't want us to forget. He's the Maker of the universe, yet he tells us he will NEVER leave us nor forsake us. What a powerful message to hold onto in the midst of a more-than-trying situation. And what a personal sentiment he wants to speak to our hearts right now.

Because our God is a personal God, he knows how much fear can overwhelm us. He knows just how deep doubt can bury its pervasive seed into our hearts. Sometimes it's so all-consuming that it's all we can see and we forget to look up.

If you're looking at your own situation right now saying there's no way you could ever find your way out, God wants you to look up. Look to him for your help—not to your own plans or crafty scenarios hoping to finagle yourself out of danger. How many times have our own plans gotten us deeper into trouble?

This verse says, "Do not be afraid or terrified because of them." I'm no Hebrew scholar. "Them" could mean people like your doctors, your boss, or your family. But it could also refer to your situation, the circumstances you can't see a way out of. That's why this verse contains a powerful reminder. God goes with you wherever you go, into whatever you're facing. He's right there beside you, holding your hand even in the midst of the fear and doubt. He loves you, and he will never leave you nor forsake you.

Yes, God's plans seem to make no sense sometimes—at least in our extremely limited human perspective. You may think you've taken into account every detail of every possibility, but God's got one thing you don't—divine perspective. He can see into your heart. He has unlimited resources at his disposal, and he's asking you to trust him. He asks you to depend of him so he can give you the strength and courage to face seemingly impossible odds.

Those of us forced to wait know exactly how hard it is not to move, not to search and struggle and fight for a way out. When your back is against the wall and you feel like you have no way out, that's when God wants you to give it all to him. Let him show you his faithfulness. He can erase all the fear and the doubt you've struggled with for so long. With his strength, you can finally be strong and courageous. Don't give up, my friend. With God on your side you can be braver than you ever thought possible.

Lord, you know how weak and helpless I feel in the face of so much fear and doubt. It feels like there's no way out, but you know better. You know just how strong and courageous I can really be, so help me to realize it with your divine perspective. Help me to claim this verse right now. I am strong and courageous. I will not be afraid or terrified because of anything, for you are my God. You go before me. You go with me every step of the way. And you will never leave me nor forsake me. Thank you for that truth, and let it sink in to my heart today. Amen.

Bonus: Read God's words to Moses and Joshua in Deuteronomy 31.

Song #2 on my YouTube playlist: "This is For Those Who Wait" by Fireflight

DAY 8

Romans 10:11

"As Scripture says, 'Anyone who believes in him will never be put to shame.'"

Let's rejoice in this truth. If we believe in God, we will never be put to shame. It's God's promise to us in his Word. So let today be the day we put all shame behind us, because we serve a God who is trustworthy. It's not foolish to believe God will come through for you.

It's so easy to beat ourselves up for trusting in God when answers don't come according to our schedule. Yet how realistic are our expectations of when God should move? Who are we to give God a timetable?

Honestly, it's only natural to be skeptical and cynical, even hesitant to trust. It's human to think that people will let you down, because they do sometimes. I'm so glad that God isn't like mankind. He's completely separate—a holy being who isn't governed my man's petty rules. He is the definition of trustworthy.

Has God given you a promise? Has he told you that he's going to come through for you in some way? Maybe through his Word, or a gentle nudge in your heart? Then it's time to start believing what he's told you. Even if it's been years since he gave you that promise.

Right now I'm sitting in a coffee shop writing this devotional years past when God gave me two specific promises. Neither of them have come to pass yet, and it's been a real struggle to keep believing. But ever since I decided to put God first in my day, and in my heart, I've started believing more than ever before.

Several years ago God spoke to my heart about how I would someday be a published author. It was after a popular teen book became a movie that I went and saw with a friend. On the way home, I practically heard God telling me I would be bigger than the author who published the book-turned-movie I just saw. It was WAY more than a nudge. The strongest I've heard God speak to me since I decided what college to attend. And you know what I did? I argued with him. Shocking, I know.

I told him I didn't want to be famous. I only wanted to earn enough in writing to make a living. I told him I never wanted the limelight and reminded him about my overwhelming fear of public speaking. But He didn't relent. And I broke down. Who was I that God would give me such a calling? To this day I have no idea. But I can still remember the trembling I felt when I surrendered to him. If that's what he wanted, he'd have to help me overcome my fears.

Be careful what you ask for, my friend. I never imagined that the journey God was about to take me on would lead to years of painful suffering with a debilitating hand injury. Not to mention all the resulting financial and relational stress that came with it. But I can tell you one thing—God is answering my prayers. I've already done one speaking engagement for my book. By my standards it went horribly. But the coordinators asked me to whip my talk into an article for their denominational magazine, *Koinonia*. So it couldn't have gone too badly.

Note that this verse doesn't say that anyone who believes in God will get exactly what they want when they want it. But it does say if you believe in God you won't be put to shame. If you step out in faith and believe the promises God has given you, there's no way you'll regret it. It's time to take that first step, and make a leap of faith.

Lord, I want to hear your promises to me today. I want to take that step of faith and believe you in spite of everything that's happening down here on Earth. You are the Maker of the universe and everything in it. In you there is no shame. Help me surrender to you today. I want to believe in you. Please, help my unbelief. Even in my doubt, help me find those seeds of faith deep in my heart. Grow those seeds of hope into belief right now, I pray. In your precious name, amen.

Bonus: Read Romans 10:9-13.

Isaiah 28:16 (the verse referenced in Romans 10:11)

So this is what the Sovereign Lord says: "See, I lay a stone in Zion, a tested stone, a precious cornerstone for a sure foundation; the one who relies on it will never be stricken with panic."

DAY 9

II Kings 3:17-18, 20

"For this is what the Lord says: You will see neither wind nor rain, yet this valley will be filled with water, and you, your cattle and your other animals will drink. This is an easy thing in the eyes of the Lord; he will also deliver Moab into your hands.

The next morning, about the time for offering the sacrifice, there it was—water flowing from the direction of Edom! And the land was filled with water."

In this complicated Old Testament story, the kings of Israel, Judah, and Edom marched through the desert against Moab on what they thought was God's errand. But their water supply dried up quicker than they anticipated, so they begged Elisha to prophesy a word from the Lord over them. These ancient kings were tired of waiting to reclaim a rebellious Moab. So they formulated a hasty plan and paid the price. Yet, God still delivered them, once they turned to him.

Waiting so long for God to do what he said he'd do can be excruciating. It all boils down to one simple word—doubt. Seeds of doubt start small and flourish at the slightest question. Did God really say this to me? Is that really what God meant?

That's when it's all too easy to start making plans on our own, especially if we think God told us to do something. This gets tricky because there are times when God wants you to make the final decision. But there are also times when God tells you to wait. Many times we fight against the call to wait. I know I did. We want to do something, move forward, and get the ball rolling. But there's still that nagging feeling in our gut that says, "Don't move." And we know it's not our idea, because we obviously don't want to wait.

So what's the surest way to overcome this cycle of doubt? The answer starts with belief. God's word is rife with reminders of how the Lord comes through for those who believe in him. Just stop and think about today's verses. If you read them in context, it all starts with Elisha's belief in God and his prophecy. But the Israelites also had to believe, or who would fight the Moabites? Even after the Israelites believed and fought the Moabites, they had to follow the fleeing enemy until they conquered all of them.

It's a powerful story that illustrates a powerful truth. Believing God is a process. It doesn't happen overnight. Belief, too, can start with a seed—a word from God, a Bible verse, or a friend's encouragement. But that's only a start. God cares more about our hearts than our circumstances. He'll use everything he can to show us the way and help us believe. Even in the middle of the desert of life, God is powerful enough to summon overflowing amounts of water out of nothing. Think of this time not just as a waiting room, but as YOUR time to wait on the Lord. Try counting how many blessings he gives you while you wait. Don't be surprised if they overflow and become blessings for others.

Lord, just as you provided water in the desert for the armies of Israel, Judah, and Edom, I ask you to show me your blessings in my parched spirit today. I am dry and thirsty, God. I need you now more than ever. Pour your Holy Spirit into my life until I'm overflowing with love and gratitude. I believe you are who you say you are, and you can do what you say you can do. Amen.

Bonus: Read the rest of the story of II Kings 3 and discover how God's blessings pour over into II Kings 4.

DAY 10

Psalm 139:11-12

"If I say, 'Surely the darkness will hide me and the light become night around me,' even the darkness will not be dark to you; the night will shine like the day, for darkness is as light to you."

Psalm 139 is one of my absolute favorite Bible passages for several different reasons. Many times in the "Waiting on the Lord" process it seems like all we're facing is darkness. This passage is about how much God knows us, how he made us, and how he has great plans for us. When I reread this passage recently, verse 12 struck me in a new light.

How many times do we want to hide from God? When I mess up, blunder into another poor decision with my own plans, or just plain get it wrong, I always want to run and hide. Yet I never feel like I can, because where on earth are you going to hide from God?

Now I know why it never works. In Bible college, my theology professor tried to explain it to me. There was one question on the test that I got wrong and I didn't understand why. It was the crux of this verse, "if I make my bed in the depths, you are there" (verse 8). My professor told me this profound truth—that we are always in God's presence. There's nowhere to hide. "For darkness is as light to you." Isn't that awesome?

If God is everywhere, even in my darkness, then it's not really as dark as it seems. Of course it still hurts when I'm at my wit's end and all I want to do is crawl into the darkness and hide. Sometimes it even feels like God's hiding from ME. But that's just another lie that the enemy wants us to believe.

If God is with us, even in our darkness, then instead of it being pitch black maybe it's really a charcoal gray with a light in the corner, waiting to burn away the darkness. "Even the darkness will not be dark to you." That means even in the blackness God is with me, holding me tight, and telling me it's going to be okay.

When I stop trying to fix it and let him take over ... it's on, baby. He's made a habit of transforming my blackest moment from charcoal gray, to light gray, to white as snow. In his own unfathomable, out-of-the-box way, he's always with us.

The journey from darkness to light is a process. The truth is, we'll always have to battle the shadowy gray areas of life. In the worst moments we need to look for the light in the blackness. To watch and pray for it. Until the day when there will be no more darkness.

Lord, I don't want to run from you anymore. I don't want to hide in the shadows. But sometimes, the blackness is all I see. God, please bring this verse to full fruition in my life today. Make my night shine like the day, for darkness is as light to you. Show me the light of your presence all around me. Lead me out of my darkness into your way everlasting. In your name I pray, amen.

Bonus: Read Psalm 139, out loud if possible.

DAY 11

II Corinthians 1:5

"For just as we share abundantly in the sufferings of Christ, so also our comfort abounds through Christ."

Paul wrote this powerful verse after he'd been in enough peril to "despair of life itself" (vs. 8). Every day people around the world wonder about the purpose of suffering. If God is good, why do we have to suffer? It's a question I still wrestle with, and you probably won't like my answer.

There's actually many reasons that we suffer pain, trials, and heartache in this life. Free will, man's depravity, the enemy—these are all part of the reason why we suffer. (Of course, the enemy has to go through God, so that brings us back to the original question.) Please understand me, friends, there's much more to the question of suffering than trying to place blame. God has his reasons. Yes, he has a plan for us, even in our suffering.

I hope you've discovered through your refocused prayers and this devotional, that God has so much to teach us in our struggles. It's the one time in our lives where we come to the end of ourselves, and God uses that to open us up to even more of his blessings than we'd ever thought possible. In the process, he wants to draw us closer to him so that we know him, and ourselves, that much better. He wants to show you the truth—you have more strength and courage than you know. Infinitely more so when you rely on Jesus as your strength.

Yet the truth about suffering goes even further beyond that. Our suffering is an opportunity to share in the suffering of Christ. The Son of God who died brutally in our place. For when we share in Christ's agony, it's a two-way street. He also shares with us abundantly, by giving us the comfort and purpose that we need.

Plus, he gives us another reason for our suffering here on earth. It's so we can share in the suffering of others. People are not blind. They can see what you're going through even if you never tell them. Many sympathize, or even empathize with your struggles. There are people out there waiting for your reaction. Maybe they're looking at what you do in order to justify their own actions. This is where the opportunity lies.

We may not even know it yet, but we have the opportunity to comfort our friends and family in their struggles. When people understand how honest you've been in your grief and anger, yet have found a way to overcome it, they're amazed. It often gives us the opportunity to point people back to Christ as their comforter. That's when all the suffering we went through turns into a blessing.

II Corinthians 1:6-7 says this, "If we are distressed, it is for your comfort and salvation; if we are comforted, it is for your comfort, which produces in you patient endurance of the same sufferings we suffer. And our hope for you is firm, because we know that just as you share in our sufferings, so also you share in our comfort."

Take the chance today to examine your surroundings, to see if there's anyone around you who's watching and waiting for you to lift them up, too. When we share in each other's suffering, we open ourselves up to receive the overwhelming comfort of Christ. Then the burden doesn't seem so heavy anymore.

Lord you know my struggles even better than I do. Help me to see exactly how I'm sharing in your sufferings today, and give me the comfort and peace you've promised in abundance. Fill me with that peace, so I can pour into others a greater measure of your love. Help me to take my eyes off of myself today, and fix them where they belong— on you. When the time is right, lead me to the people you want me to minister to. For yours is the glory forever, amen.

Bonus: II Corinthians 1:1-10

DAY 12

Psalm 27:13-14

"I remain confident of this: I will see the goodness of the Lord in the land of the living. Wait for the Lord; be strong and take heart and wait for the Lord."

So often when we're waiting on the Lord, it feels like we're on shaky ground. Like our feet aren't firmly planted anywhere and we're tumbling through outer darkness. And it makes us panic. People do irrational and impulsive things when they panic. They scramble around to find a solution—*any* solution. We go into a fight-or-flight response. Yet the more we scramble around, the *less* confident we feel. Especially if we're looking for a human solution when we really need to be looking up for the heavenly one.

One of my very best friends works at a drug and alcohol rehab center for teenage girls. Every now and then a girl just up and runs away, even though the facility isn't in the safest part of town. Why would a teenage girl risk the horrors of the street when she could stay in the safety of a supervised rehab program? My friend thinks it's because of this fight-or-flight response. In an intense program like drug and alcohol rehabilitation, you are forced to face the issues that brought you to the program. They're not pretty, and there are no easy solutions.

When we look to our own wisdom for the solution to our problems, that's when we start to lose confidence. Because the only real solution to our problems is in the Lord, even if that means waiting on him. It's time to lift our eyes from the mess and look up to God, where our help comes from. That's where we can find real confidence that he will come through for us.

It's all too tempting to get distracted by the struggles of life we deal with. That's why this verse has two parts. It tells us to remain confident in God, but also to "be strong and take heart" as we wait for the Lord. Because that's the only way to remain confident that God will come through at just the right time. Being strong and taking heart as you wait on the Lord could mean it's time to change your priorities.

Reach for God. Be alone with him. Let him show you his solutions through his Word. In my darkest times God urged me to write out key Bible verses on note cards so I could have them ready when I needed them again. Be open to how God wants to speak to you. Because once you know him intimately, you'll not only find more confidence and strength in God, but in yourself as well.

Lord, I want to be confident in you, but it's so hard with everything I'm dealing with right now. Help me to see your goodness in my circumstances today. Lift my eyes to you, where my true help comes from. Help me to be strong and take heart. Speak to me about how I can draw closer to you, where I'll find the confidence I so desperately need. Even now I claim that confidence. You will come through for me as only you can. Amen.

Bonus: Psalm 27, Isaiah 49:8-13

DAY 13

Jeremiah 31:3-4a

The Lord appeared to us in the past, saying: "I have loved you with an everlasting love; I have drawn you with unfailing kindness. I will build you up again."

Sometimes it's good to remember what God has done for us in the past. He's sheltered us, provided for us, and loved us no matter what. Even if we don't have a perfectly seamless walk with the Lord to look back on, God was still with us. He has brought us this far and he will see us through. You can count on it. But now is not the time to rest on past laurels, or put on our rose-colored glass to compare the past with the present. That's not the purpose of remembering—at least not God's purpose.

Living in the past can be dangerous, because we don't always remember it accurately. Our memories are fuzzy and fleeting, based on impressions and highlighted information which isn't always a true picture of what happened. It's great to go back and remember all the marvelous things God's done for you. Just don't stay there. Don't live in the past just because the present hurts too much. Everything that has happened in your life has brought you to where you are today. Why? So you can change and grow into something even more beautiful in your

Father's sight. Because he looks at our heart. Only he knows its true potential.

That's why I love the beginning of verse 4, "I will build you up again." No matter what you're up against right now, God has this promise for you. He will build you up again. And the truth is, once you let him rebuild you from the inside out, you'll find more freedom than you've ever known.

In my past I believed that I was the only Christian missing the boat. Everyone else around me seemed happy, fulfilled, and full of faith in God. Not me. I was completely insecure, always worrying and doubting. Too many times I tried to put on that happy face, but eventually it cracked wide open and I had to face the truth. I wasn't putting God first in my life. I wasn't letting him build me up. Instead I was trying to build myself up high enough to reach him. Now it's so obvious that's what I was doing, but then it didn't feel so good.

Boy, am I ever glad that God knocked me down a peg or two. I needed it. Badly. I had to get to a place where I was so completely desperate for him that I finally turned to him first. He was all I had left. I started putting him first, rather than wallow in misery for the rest of the day. If I missed my morning time with God, I could feel it. I started in the Psalms, because the Psalmists knew how I felt. They wrote about ultimate worship and ultimate despair. Yet they found a way to point out the uplifting parts of their despair. If you're struggling to find hope, trying reading through the Psalms. God is waiting there.

Lord, I want to find hope again. I've wrestled with darkness for so long that hope seems like a faraway concept. I don't want to cling to things that aren't of you. I want to be close to you and hope again. Help me to put you first today. Help me to focus on you and open my heart to hear your response. Build me up again, starting today, I pray. Amen.

Bonus: Read Psalm 1.

DAY 14

Isaiah 26:3

"You will keep in perfect peace those whose minds are steadfast, because they trust in you."

Simple but eloquent. To me this verse explains the whole complicated process of "perfect peace" in a nutshell. Everything about this verse, the "perfect peace" and "steadfast mind" we long to achieve, is summed up in that last clause. Especially if you make it personal. "Because *we* trust in you."

I believe that the Bible is a great source of wisdom, but it's also a great tool for prayer. I know many people are so careful not to misquote the Bible or add to its words, which is a good goal unto itself. But the purpose of the Bible isn't just so it can sit on a shelf collecting dust until we need to reference it again. The Bible is meant to be used as a tool to combat the everyday battles we face. That means it's time to make it personal. After reading Beth Moore's book *Praying God's Word*, I believe you'll be convinced of just how powerful the Bible can be when we use it as a prayer tool. We can turn our favorite Bible verses into personal prayers, just by changing a few pronouns.

If this verse speaks to you like it does to me, I challenge you to make it your own. Write it down on a note card for the next time you head-butt against something that throws you into inner turmoil. Commit it to memory, highlight it in your Bible, post a note on your phone, or whatever you need to do to remind yourself of the truth God's speaking to you. If a verse resonates with you, God knows you'll need it again. I guarantee it.

The point of this verse hinges on trusting in God. Above everything else. Don't wait for God to deliver you from the storm before you start trusting in him. That's the time to praise him for deliverance. But right now, in the middle of your darkest night, God's telling you to trust him to see you through. He is your Father, and he is so much bigger than your storm.

I heard a great example of this on the radio the other day. A son came to his mother saying he was afraid of the monster growls he heard at night. His brother pointed to the toy chest and said, "It's the dinosaur toy that roars." Mom turned off the sound on the dino toy, and suddenly there were no more monster growls for her son to be afraid of. God is much like that. He's infinitely bigger than any of our battles, and he wants us to come to him with our fears. He wants to show us just how much BIGGER he is than anything we could ever be afraid of.

Once we finally learn to trust him he's waiting to give us that perfect peace we long for, and to make our minds steadfast. Don't get me wrong, trusting God and finding his perfect peace is definitely a process. It's a process that begins with that first step—finding a way to trust him even when we don't understand. He's bigger than we can ever know, and he's got our back.

Lord, I long for your perfect peace today, but it seems unattainable with the struggles I'm dealing with. Help me to find a way to trust in you. Show me just how much bigger you are than everything in this world. Help me to keep my mind steadfast. Show me that perfect peace I long for as I learn to trust in you. Speak those truths to my heart today, I pray. Amen.

Bonus: Isaiah 26:1-15

Recommended reading: Beth Moore, *Praying God's Word*

DAY 15

Genesis 28:15

"I am with you and will watch over you wherever you go, and I will bring you back to this land. I will not leave you until I have done what I have promised you."

This was the promise God gave to Jacob as he showed him the vision of the heavenly staircase with angels ascending and descending to Earth. This was also right after God promised Jacob numerous descendants and numerous blessings. All before he ever married Leah or Rachel. But none of this happened until Jacob started on the road of obedience. His father, Isaac, told him where to go and who to marry, and Jacob set off on his journey. God met Jacob on the way, giving him his own promises and blessings.

I don't know about you, but personally, I have a tough time with obedience. It's not a natural inclination for me to obey anyone else's commands. In fact, I really dislike being told what to do. That's probably why the area of obedience is something God has had to hammer me with over and over again. In the process, I've learned that submitting to God doesn't equal less freedom. In fact, it means more freedom for me. Freedom from worry, fear, and doubt. Once I give something over to him he carries my burdens. Even more than that, this verse promises us freedom from loneliness.

It's freeing to know that God is with you, "wherever you go," no matter what. He will watch over you and, if you follow him, he will not leave you empty handed. He'll do exactly what he's promised you.

We've been going over God's promises in the past few days. I hope God has spoken to you or reminded you about specific promises he's made to you that you're not to give up on. Regardless, this verse is it's own promise to you. We all feel alone sometimes. No matter how lonely you feel, you are never alone. God is always with you. He watches over you. He's promised us an eternity with him when we trust in his Son, so that means he will never leave us.

Lord, help me to feel your presence in my life today. Show me all the ways that you are watching over me, and bring me back to your promises. Holy Spirit, whisper these truths deep into my heart—you will never leave me or forsake me, and you will do what you've promised me. Seal those promises on my heart today, I pray. Amen.

Bonus: Genesis 28:1-15

DAY 16

Ephesians 4:17

"So I tell you this, and insist on it in the Lord, that you must no longer live as the Gentiles do, in the futility of their thinking."

Paul is adamant here that once we turn our lives over to Christ, we should no longer rely on our own thoughts. Yes, that means it's time to fully turn your thought life over to God. The mind is a battlefield, and Jesus wants us to find freedom there, too. That's one of the many reasons he died for us, so that we don't have to live in our sinful minds any longer. We don't have to keep playing the litany of negativity over and over again in our heads until we've got the script memorized. Those negative thoughts that hold us captive are not of God. They are lies from the enemy meant to keep us in our prison cells—bound to our own desires and failures. The truth is God wants to set your mind free to think on him and how much he loves you.

Turning our thoughts from the enemy's lies to God's truths is an everyday process. A struggle even. That's why I'm so glad you're reading this book. Keep soaking up the powerful Word of God. It's the only way to break down those strongholds. And when we find ourselves in the middle of heartbreak, the loss of a loved one, or a seemingly insurmountable health issue, God's word is the only thing we can truly cling to.

Recently I had a friend whose mother was in and out of the hospital with unexplained seizures. This was about the same time my dad was struck by a car and hospitalized for two months. My friend and I exchanged encouragement through Facebook messages, but his mother only got worse while my dad started to recover. Eventually my friend's mother died twice. Once until she was brain-dead, and then finally her body gave out and she went to be with the Lord. My friend was so devastated that he didn't know what to do. He reached out through Facebook, sharing his struggle and that he was going to put himself in the hospital on suicide watch.

So my husband and I prayed to combat the enemy that was battling for control of my friend's thoughts. He was in the middle of complete darkness, the kind that wears you down until you feel you have nothing left. The only way out of such darkness is to cling to a ray of hope—a pinprick of light. God's word is that light, the truth that we need to find our way out of darkness. Start reading and meditating on his word. Build up your arsenal now, so that when the day of evil comes you can stand firm.

Lord, speak your words of truth and life into my heart and mind today. Illuminate the shadowy corners of my mind and expose the lies I've held on to for far too long. Help me to find the truth in your Word to combat each and every one of the lies I tell myself. You sent your Son to die for me so that I could be set free in every area of my life. Set my mind free today, by the power of your sacrifice, Jesus. Amen.

Bonus: II Corinthians 10:3-6, Ephesians 4:1-24

DAY 17

Ephesians 6:13

"Therefore put on the full armor of God, so that when the day of evil comes, you may be able to stand your ground, and after you have done everything, to stand."

This is only the introductory verse to the next four verses that tell us exactly how to put on the full armor of God. We are going to need God's armor now and in the future. The enemy does not want us to succeed, be happy, follow God, and worship him with all of our hearts. He will do anything he can think of to take us down. Yet, God is always in control. He won't let us be tempted beyond what we can handle. Plus, he gives us powerful weapons to combat the enemy and show us who's really on our side. Here's where I'd like to suggest two things for you to do with these verses about the armor of God found in Ephesians 6:14-18.

1. Memorize vs. 14-17: Do whatever you need to do to commit these verses to memory, make notecards, recite them to yourself, make up a song for these words. You will need these verses again. If the battle isn't already at your doorstep, it'll come. As you grow closer to the Lord, the enemy will take notice. God's words of truth are the best weapons of warfare against the lies of the deceiver.

2. Personalize these verses: Meditate on the pieces of armor. Picture yourself strapping them in place. Discover what each part means specifically to you. Fortify your shield of faith by reminding yourself how much you believe in God, or exactly how he's been faithful to you. Put on your own helmet of salvation, and pick up those verses you memorized as your sword of truth. Pray about it. Seek God and ask him to reveal exactly where you need to be fortified.

I've had these verses memorized for a long time, almost since I found Jesus years ago. In fact, I recite them to myself almost every day. Why? Because my life isn't always sunshine and roses. I've been battling the enemy for a long time. Sometimes I get tired of fighting and it feels like I'll never win. That's when these verses have become life preservers. They remind me that I CAN fight and that God is always on my side. No matter what happens, in the end God's always going to win. Every battle that I fight brings me closer to regaining the high ground and reclaiming the life that God has for me. So don't give up, my friends. God is on your side, too.

Lord, buckle the belt of truth around my waist today. Put the breastplate of righteousness in place. Fit my feet with the readiness that only comes from your gospel of peace. In addition to this, I take up the shield of faith with which I can extinguish all the flaming arrows of the evil one. I put on the helmet of salvation to guard my mind, and take up the sword of the spirit—which is your word of truth. Help me to stand my ground today. I can do all things through Christ who strengthens me. Amen.

Bonus: Read Ephesians 6:10-18. Memorize each verse and each weapon of warfare. Pray these words as often as you need to, and personalize these verses so you can understand them and use them to the fullest.

DAY 18

Jeremiah 10:23

"Lord, I know that people's lives are not their own; it is not for them to direct their steps."

Even though I know there's so much truth in this, every instinct within me reels against this concept. It's a constant battle to put God's will above my own plans. Nonetheless, it's a battle I must fight. Jeremiah said this in the midst of ruin, destruction, and captivity—a horrible time in Israel's history. Yet he had a word from God and was prophesying to the Israelites to pack up and leave. I don't know if the battle was upon them yet, but I do know that this is the first line of Jeremiah's prayer for his people as they flee.

There comes a point for each of us when we finally come to the end of our own strength. But that's no reason to sink further into despair. When you're out of options and your back is against the wall, that's when there's only one option left.

Complete and utter surrender.

Total surrender is not as defeating as it seems. Surrender is a place where God is waiting to take your hand and show you that he really is enough for you. He's your Heavenly Father and he wants to lead you into something great. He wants to strengthen and encourage you and prove just how much he loves you.

Sometimes the hardest battles are the ones we fight within ourselves. Believe me, I know how difficult it is to let go and trust someone you've never seen. Just because you can't see him doesn't mean he isn't with you. He's just more subtle than we'd prefer. God is in that glorious sunset. What about those unexplained moments of peace or a truth that resonates deep within you? God is speaking to you. He's reaching out to you. What will your response be?

It's time to let go.

Be still and know that God is with you.

It's time to stop placing blame and let God take over.

But that also means that it's time to trust him, even when things are so ridiculously hard that you have no idea what's going to happen next. You don't have to worry anymore, God knows exactly what's coming. He will prepare your heart for it. In fact, that's one of the great purposes of waiting on the Lord. If you surrender to him, he can change your heart. That's what he longs to do. He's in the heart-changing business, after all.

Lord, I'm finally starting to realize that my life is not my own. I want to surrender completely to you, but I don't know how. So I'm starting with today. Help me to find the strength to let go of all of the burdens I've been carrying. I know you will take care of them. They are in good hands. Speak to me right now and show me that you are with me. I want to be still and feel just how much you love me. Today, I want to start trusting in you fully. Bring me back to this place of surrender when I start taking on too much again. Change my heart today, as only you can, God. Amen.

DAY 19

II Kings 4:1-3

"The wife of a man from the company of the prophets cried out to Elisha, "Your servant my husband is dead, and you know that he revered the Lord. But now his creditor is coming to take my two boys as his slaves. Elisha replied to her, 'How can I help you? Tell me, what do you have in your house?'

"Your servant has nothing there at all," she said, "except a small jar of olive oil." Elisha said, "Go around and ask all your neighbors for empty jars. Don't ask for just a few."

This verse starts out with injustice heaped upon an already tragic event. Like this poor woman hadn't suffered enough when her husband died, but now creditors are threatening to take her two sons as slaves? So she ran straight to the person who she knew had the ear of the Lord, Elisha the prophet. He comes up with a ludicrous solution. If you haven't read this story before, Elisha prophesies over the multitude of jars this woman collects and they all fill with enough oil to sell for the money needed for her husband's creditors.

If I were this woman, I know I'd have a hard time just going along with Elisha's plan. I'd probably be trailing along behind him, asking him why I needed so many jars. My favorite part of this little seven verse story is what Elisha tells her, "Don't ask for just a few." How many times are we tempted to ask for so little from God? Do we not have enough faith to ask for more than "a few?" If we truly believe in a big God, who is bigger than anything we could ever face, why aren't we asking him to come through for us in a big way?

Maybe it's because we don't want to be disappointed. Or we don't want God to tell us no. But part of believing in a big God means that we have to trust him to know just how and when to answer. And unfortunately, he doesn't explain everything to us beforehand. Since I'm that girl who always wants to know why, this is the hardest part for me to swallow. That's where faith comes in. If you read the next verses, 4-7, you'll see that God does come through for this widow in a big and miraculous way. It's a path I bet she never expected. Once God provided more than enough oil for her and her sons to sell to pay her debt, she knew the answers to everything she'd been wondering about.

Part of having big faith is being able to trust God long enough to wait for him to come through for you. Even when it feels like he's not answering you, believe that he's working all things for your good. Because that's just the kind of God he is. What can you trust God with today in a big way?

Lord, I don't want to have little faith anymore. I want to believe you'll come through for me in the big ways, not just the small ways I've always known. Expand my horizons today. Take me deeper into your Word and this journey of faith than I ever thought possible. Help me to learn to trust you for more and to seek you in prayer about every big obstacle in my way. Amen.

* * *

Bonus: A Personal Testimony

When I wrote this devotional, I had no idea exactly where God would take my writing journey. I just knew I needed to believe him and trust him for the rest. While editing this day's devotional weeks after it was written, I received an unexpected answer to one of the big things I'd been waiting on the Lord for. Over a year ago I received a contract for my debut YA novel *The Nexis Secret* from a small press. I thought it was a dream come true, but it quickly turned into a disaster. After ten months of no communication and missed deadlines, my publisher and I parted ways. I was back to square one.

I told the story to an editor friend of mine who mentored me in a short story group several years ago. She had her own small press, but decided to change her business to a hybrid imprint where she freelances her editing services and lets authors use her label for promotion. When she heard I was looking to go indie, she immediately offered to bring me into this new program. So now I have a professional editor who wants to move up my release date so she can promote *The Nexis Secret* at a conference.

I know that this never would've happened if I hadn't listened to God and waited on him when he told me to wait. I don't know what the future holds, but I feel an overwhelming sense of peace that God's hand is all over this. That alone gives me the courage to face the unknown. Because if God is for us, who can be against us?

DAY 20

I Corinthians 1:30

"It is because of him that you are in Christ Jesus, who has become for us wisdom from God—that is our righteousness, holiness, and redemption."

This is another great verse to jot down on a note card, commit to memory, and pray over your own life. If you're anything like me, then there may be times you're tempted to bargain with God. Or there may be times you think you need to show God just how good you can be on your own. My friend, let me tell you the truth. There's no way you can ever be good enough to earn the stamp of "righteous" on your own. And without righteousness, you can never be holy and redeemed, either.

Aren't you glad God sent his Son to die in our place? The blood that Jesus shed for us on the cross became our righteousness. His sacrifice trumps our own wisdom. That's how he became "for us wisdom from God." Meaning we don't have to keep trying to earn our place in the kingdom of heaven. A way has already been made for us. All we have to do is trust in the Son of God who took our place and died so we could live righteous, holy, and redeemed lives. Today. Right now.

Can you feel the weight lifting off your shoulders? Can you feel the freedom Jesus' sacrifice brings us?

Don't get me wrong, we still need to strive to be good citizens in God's kingdom and be more like Jesus every day. In fact, we should keep him in mind as our ultimate example. But in that instance, our goals are different. We aren't trying to earn favor with God, or the Lord's favor over our friends and fellow Christians. Striving to be more like Jesus should come naturally out of our love for him. Being like Jesus means humbling ourselves as a servant of God and a servant to mankind, just like our Savior did in his time here on earth.

That's why I love this verse so much. It takes the pressure off of me. I don't have to keep trying to be what everyone else thinks I should be. As a natural-born people pleaser, believe me that's been a tough lesson for me to learn. That's why I love living for God only and cultivating my relationship with him. It doesn't matter any more if people aren't happy with everything I do. There's no way you can please everyone. But if you follow God and let Jesus be your righteousness, holiness, and redemption, then you can always know you're pleasing the most important person on earth and in heaven.

Jesus, thank you for coming to earth, living among us, and dying in my place. I know you came to set me free from trying to do everything on my own. So today I ask you to be my righteousness, holiness, and redemption. I know that apart from you, none of this is truly possible. Only your sacrifice, the blood you shed for me, can make me righteous, holy, and redeemed. You did it all for me, and took my place. Today I thank you for your sacrifice, and ask you to help me live fully in the freedom you bought for me for the rest of my days. Amen.

Bonus: Song #1 on my YouTube playlist, MercyMe's "Greater"

DAY 21

Psalm 27:5

"For in the day of trouble he will keep me safe in his dwelling; he will hide me in the shelter of his sacred tent and set me high upon a rock."

If you've heard the adage, "Nothing about God is safe, but yet we are completely safe in him," and wondered what in the world that meant, you're not alone. This verse is the closest I've found to explaining the mystifying truth of God's safety net. Let's face it, nothing about setting me "high upon a rock" sounds very safe. Yet sometimes that's the furthest place from danger. Because if God is sheltering us in his sacred tent in the day of trouble, what safer place could we ever find on our own? That's the promise found in this verse, that "he will keep me safe in his dwelling."

The problem lies in what we think is safe versus what God knows to be safe. Human nature tells us to stockpile our money in case of emergency, to try any pill necessary to keep us healthy, and find happiness in companionship even if it's only temporary. None of those things are bad in and of themselves. But if we trust in any of those things before we trust in God, there's a problem. Because God wants all of our hearts, not just the scraps. He doesn't want to be tenth on the list of emergency contacts. He wants to be number one. And he deserves to be number one.

God knows all things, including what we truly need. He is most concerned about our hearts, and he uses the circumstances of life to shape our character to its fullest potential. Even if the shaping hurts. Why does he let things happen that hurt us? Because he loves us enough to want the absolute best for us. If we trust in his best, then we shouldn't settle for anything less. Even when that frustrates us and takes us out of our comfort zones.

Here's the challenge for today—stop wrestling with God to fit him into your schedule. Take a moment to listen to what God's telling you, and get on board with his design. Trust me, I've been there so many times. Once you relinquish the reins, you'll be forever glad you did. Then, "in the day of trouble" you'll find yourself safe in God's arms. He is always with us to shelter and protect us.

God, I try so hard to find safety that sometimes I look for it in all the wrong places. I want to stop trying to do things my way. But I need you to speak to me. Show me how to let go of my agenda, my priorities, and my schedule. Replace them with your priorities for my life, and help me to see the next step in the journey. You know my heart, and you know how much I want to do your will. Holy Spirit keep me safe, comfort me, give me peace, and shape my heart until my will becomes your will. I'm letting go today, and letting you take charge of keeping me safe from now on. Lead me on your path, I pray. Amen.

Bonus: Read Psalm 27.

DAY 22

Isaiah 45:2-3

"I will go before you and will level the mountains; I will break down gates of bronze and cut through bars of iron. I will give you the treasures of darkness, riches stored in secret places, so that you may know that I am the Lord, the God of Israel, who summons you by name."

This is one of God's many promises to you, just as it was to Israel. Through the prophet Isaiah, God promised to restore his people, Israel, to their homeland, their former glory. He even promised to use an ungodly king to fulfill this promise. If God can restore a whole nation using ungodly people, how much more can God restore you?

You may think this is easy for me to say, but I can assure you it's not. I do not live in the lap of luxury, nor do I come from a godly home. My parents divorced when I was four because of drug and alcohol problems. When I was seven my mother married a schizophrenic man who frequently missed his meds. My childhood was not always safe, nor was it easy. I found Jesus at age fourteen and later went to Bible college at seventeen—but my life didn't immediately get easier. I've always had to struggle and fight for what I know is right. Sometimes even against my own family.

I don't share this for you to feel sorry for me. In fact, I don't tell most people this for that very reason. I'm sharing my past with you because I want you to know that it IS possible for you to overcome anything. No matter what you've been through, or what you're going through right now, you CAN overcome it. Because God is with you. He will level mountains for you, just like he did for me. Because of my childhood, I feel God's call to write books for teens who live with similar issues.

God can help you overcome the battles you've faced in your life. He's there to help you with the ones you're facing right now. He wants to break down all the barriers for you, even gates of bronze and bars of iron. He will go with you, but you have to fight the battle. You still need to be obedient to whatever God is speaking to you. Even if you're afraid, you can surrender that to God. Let him use it to give you the courage you need to keep pressing on and moving forward until together you've gained the victory. He will give you the treasures you fought for in the darkness. All the riches he bestows can be found in the secret places of your heart, where God calls you by name.

Lord, I claim this promise from Isaiah over my life right now. Go before me today and prepare the way. Level the mountains, break down the gates of bronze and cut through bars of iron. Give me the courage to keep fighting, to keep trusting in you for my strength. Speak to the secret places of my heart that are dark and unsure. Call me by name, so that I may know you are the Lord. Amen.

Bonus: Read Isaiah 45:1-13, 15-19, 22-25.

DAY 23

Romans 8:37

"No, in all these things we are more than conquerors through him who loved us."

It's one thing to read this verse, and another to actually believe the powerful truth—we are more than conquerors because God loves us. The proof that God loves us rests in Jesus. God sent his own Son—his right hand, the second person of the trinity—to die in our place. So we could be forgiven. So our slate can be wiped clean. Because we are forgiven through Christ's sacrifice, we have reason to celebrate. We are more than conquerors over whatever happens to us in this life.

Believe this with me today, we are more than conquerors in Christ Jesus. Say it to anything and everything that comes against you or brings you down right now. Speak out loud to whatever you're facing:

I am more than a conqueror over the fear and doubt in my mind.

I am more than a conqueror over this stupid sin that keeps calling my name.

I am more than a conqueror over the betrayal of a loved one.

I am more than a conqueror over this illness that ravages my body.

I am more than a conqueror over the anger that churns inside me.

I am more than a conqueror over the wrong that someone else committed against me.

I am more than a conqueror over anything the enemy throws at me.

Because I have Jesus Christ on my side. He loves me and nothing can separate me from his love.

It's time to let go of anything that keeps you captive, whether it's in your heart, mind, or body. If you've accepted Jesus into your heart, you don't have to live in bondage to anything ever again. But do not be fooled. Even Christians can live in bondage. So many times we think that only unsaved people live in bondage. Beth Moore puts it this way, "A Christian is held captive by anything that hinders the abundant and effective Spirit-filled life God planned for him or her."

If you don't feel set free, or feel like you're missing the abundance that other Christians seem to have, then maybe you're bound to something you're not fessing up to. It could be something like anger or not fully trusting in God because of past or present circumstances. Or it could be a sin issue you've never been able to kick. I'm not asking you to over-analyze yourself or to try to be perfect, because those are traps in and of themselves. I'm just asking you to be honest with yourself.

Now is the time to take care of it. Now is the time to say, "I am more than a conqueror over anything that seeks to separate me from my Father." Don't stay locked up in your inner cell anymore. Surrender yourself to your Maker and proclaim the victory he gives you.

Lord, I embrace your Word today, that I am more than a conqueror because you love me. Help me to proclaim the victory over every obstacle I'm facing, because you are with me. If there's anything holding me captive, gently illuminate the truth. Show me how to overcome so I can live for you and walk in your abundance. Make me more than a conqueror today, for in you I find victory. Amen.

Bonus: Romans 8:1-4, 31b-39

Recommended reading: Beth Moore, *Breaking Free* and *Breaking Free Day by Day* devotional

DAY 24

II Corinthians 5:17

"Therefore, if anyone is in Christ, he is a new creation; the old has gone, the new has come!"

If you're feeling stuck in a rut, then this verse is screaming out your name. It's one of those fabulous Bible verses with its own exclamation point! As a writer, I've been told time and time again not to use an exclamation point unless I REALLY mean it. God means what he says in this verse. You can count on it!

Because Christ died for us we are not only set free from captivity, but we are also new creations in him. Glorious and radiant new creations, I might add. That's one of the many reasons Jesus shed his blood on the cross for us, so we could be washed clean. Pure as can be.

So why do we cling to the old nature—wandering around on our own? Because we're human. News flash. No one on this earth is perfect apart from God. But in him, we are made new.

Isn't that great news? You don't have to hang on to everything that drags you down anymore. Just throw it at the feet of Jesus and he will wash it away. If you're feeling stuck and don't know where to start, just come to Jesus. Come to his Word and lay your troubles, sorrows, and burdens at his feet. Do this as often as you need to. Once a day, multiple times a day—it doesn't matter. He is always with you, ready to make you new again.

It's not too late to be made new. If you're feeling lost, far from hope, or far from grace, I want you to know that you're not very far from Jesus. Because he goes with you wherever you go, and he walks with you wherever you walk. It's not too late to ask for forgiveness. Ask him to make you clean and reconcile you with God. He's God's Son. He can do it.

We all need to be renewed sometimes. Most of us need to be renewed every day. When I was suffering through my debilitating work injury, I needed a fresh touch of Jesus every morning. On the most painful days I needed to be made new multiple times a day. During that time I read at least four devotionals a day and poured through as many Psalms as I could get through in one day. Why? Because that's how much I needed Jesus to come and make me new. That's also why this verse is on its own note card. I know I'll need it often.

If you're as hungry, desperate, and thirsty as I was, now is the time to submit yourself to Jesus so he can make you new. He will meet you at your point of need. Wherever that is. He wants to show you that you're a new creation in him.

Lord, help me to see that I am a new creation in you. Right now I submit myself to you. Remove the old me with the thoughts and habits I've been walking around with for so long. Jesus, make me new today. Renew my mind, fill me with your strength when I am weak. I rejoice that I am a new creation! Thank you for making me new in your name, Jesus. Amen.

Bonus: II Corinthians 5:15-21, 12:9-10. If you haven't already done so, consider adding a Psalm a day to your daily time with God.

DAY 25

Luke 22:42

"Father, if you are willing, take this cup from me; yet not my will, but yours be done."

Have you ever felt like Jesus did in the Garden of Gethsemane on the eve of the cross? If even the Son of God felt weary and anguished enough to pray this prayer, how can we not relate? This is an honest prayer. A prayer that says, "Hey God, this stinks. The path I'm on right now is awful and horrible and I don't want it anymore." Yet it's a prayer with two parts. One side that acknowledges the horrors Jesus was about to face, and another side that knew exactly what his blood would purchase. Our freedom. Forever. Once and for all.

There are many times where I could only pray the first half of this prayer. Like in the middle of the night when the couch was the only place I could sleep with a bit less pain. Even now, as I'm writing this day's devotion, pain has flared up in my right hand. I thought about putting off today's writing time and letting myself rest until tomorrow. And there are times when that is the best thing for me to do. But not today. I feel God urging me to press on through the pain.

That's the essence of the second part of Jesus' prayer in the garden, "Yet not my will, but yours be done." There is a purpose for us even in the middle of our pain, our trials, and our suffering. Our God is not a god who leaves people to rot. He proved that by sending his Son to die for you on the cross. He, and he alone, can turn anything that seems unbearable into something good. That's just who he is. If he can turn the death of his Son into a resurrection story full of life, then he can turn whatever darkness you're stuck in back to light. He's just that good.

When you're hurting, believe me, I know it's hard to pray the last part of this prayer. But it is the most critical part. God wants you to come to him with everything. He wants you to be open and honest with him. He already knows everything you're going through. But he also wants you to let him be your Father and to let him be in control. Because he is bigger than the obstacles we're facing today. With God we can overcome them and not only live to tell the tale, but bring others along the journey with us. Will you let him be your Father so he can guide you straight into his will?

Father, I want to be honest with you today. You know exactly what I'm up against, and exactly how I'm handling everything. It hurts, and I can't face it alone. I want you to take this cup from me today. Yet I know you have a bigger plan for me, just like you did for Jesus. Because we are both your children now. So be my Father today and take control of my situation. Let your will be done, on earth as it is in heaven. Amen.

Bonus: Luke 22:39-46

DAY 26

"For you did not receive a spirit that makes you a slave again to fear, but you received the Spirit of sonship. And by him we cry, 'Abba, Father.'"

Romans 8 is a chapter full of rich truths. Camped in the middle between "there is now no condemnation for those who are in Christ Jesus" (v.1) and "we are more than conquerors" (v.37) is verse 15—a jewel of a truth. You can overcome condemnation and become more than a conqueror of fear when you accept your rightful place in God's kingdom. Fear really does have the power to enslave us and defeat us. Especially when it's combined with condemnation. Thank God that he's given us a way to overcome fear.

My favorite thing about this verse is how God uses our status as children in his kingdom to reassure us and bring us comfort, which is the opposite of fear. If you're being assaulted by Satan's lies today you need to examine this truth carefully. God wants you to know that you are his child. If you've accepted Christ, then the Holy Spirit dwells within you. And the Spirit of God doesn't live in fear and trembling at the enemy's hand. No matter what happens in our physical or spiritual battles, God will always be victorious over the enemy. Satan doesn't want you to believe that God always wins, but he does. In fact, the enemy doesn't want you to believe he even exists. Why? Because you can't fight an enemy you don't think is there. Then you may never know the riches God has in store for you.

If we are God's children then we are his heirs, even "co-heirs with Christ" (v.17). Verse 17 goes on to say "if indeed we share in his sufferings in order that we may also share in his glory." It's amazing to me that we can share in the glory of God's Son if we also share in his sufferings. That doesn't mean ignoring it or pretending like the cross never happened. It means accepting nothing but the truth. The whole truth. While tragic and unimaginably painful, Jesus suffered and died for a purpose. To cleanse us from our sins once and for all, so we could accept this verse and be God's children and co-heirs with Christ.

But don't forget about the resurrection. After three days Jesus rose from the grave, walked among his people, and ascended into glory. That's the whole truth. When suffering happens in this life, most people blame God first. Yes, I've been among them many times. We ask why won't God relieve our suffering? Why won't he take away the pain or fix the situation? Those are the questions the enemy wants us to ask.

God wants us to ask a different set of questions. What is God going to do in the midst of my suffering? How is he going to turn this around for his glory? Since he is with me, how can I overcome this? Ultimately, the lessons God teaches us through pain, suffering, heartache, and upheaval, are all lessons that eventually turn into blessings like strength, overcoming fear, trust in God, and drawing closer to him. They're not just blessings for us, either. It's amazing the testimony we give to those we didn't even know were watching. Through suffering we not only become better people, but we can draw so much closer to God.

Romans 8 is all about defeating the enemy on every battlefield. But it all starts in the battlefield of the mind. A little change of perspective can change everything. When those doubts and fears come rushing to your mind, remember this verse. Turn the fear around and ask how God as your heavenly Father can overcome. Then sit back and watch him work.

Father, thank you that you've called me your child and given me the Holy Spirit. Refresh and revive my soul. Make me no longer a slave to fear. Show me my place in your kingdom. Help me to see your hand at work, even in my pain. I want to share in the suffering of Christ like a brother, and share in his glory too. Change my perspective, Daddy God. Help me to see the whole truth and how you're really hard at work in my life. Amen.

Bonus: Romans 8

Song #3 on my YouTube playlist No Longer Slaves by Bethel Music

DAY 27

Ephesians 3:12

"In him and through faith in him we may approach God with freedom and confidence."

It's vitally important to remember that we can approach God with confidence. No matter who you are or what you've done, if you've accepted Jesus into your heart, then you are God's child and can come to him with anything. You have the freedom to tell him everything you're struggling with—exactly what's on your heart. He will listen. He wants you to approach him with full freedom and confidence.

Today I went on a nice long walk with a friend and she was telling me how she broke down and cried out to God for direction in her life. But the funny thing was how she qualified it, saying she knew she didn't deserve such grace. How many times do we all think this, that we don't deserve God's grace? That we don't deserve for him to answer our prayers? Please understand me, none of us deserve anything from God. But God is not a god of the deserving. He is a God of grace and mercy. He knows just how much we need him. Now he wants US to know how much we need him, too.

It's okay to cry out to God with whatever is on your mind. It's okay to ask him to help you. He is your father and he longs to help you.

Usually that's by showing you the next step or encouraging you on your journey. Because for God it's all about the process. It's in the process of learning to trust him that we draw closer to him. It's in the process of drawing closer to him that we get to know him better. It's in the process of getting to know him better that we receive more blessings than we could ever imagine and a greater sensitivity to the sound of his voice in our lives.

Don't get me wrong, I love it when God speaks to me in big booming ways. But that's only happened three times in my life so far—the call to salvation, the call to Bible college, and the call to write. Even then, not all of those directives were clear as a bell. They were just a starting point for a new journey. Some pretty big events are left off that list. But in those things I had to find God in a smaller way—in a still small voice nudging me forward, a door of opportunity closing, a verse in the Bible, a song, or a friend.

Now that I know how many ways he can speak to me, I finally understand that I can approach God with freedom and confidence. I may not always get the answer I want, but I'll get the next step that I need. Because when we come to God with our needs, he's always faithful to meet them.

Father, give me the courage and the faith to be able to approach you with confidence today. I know I don't deserve a touch from you, but I really need one right now. I need to you to wrap your arms around me and whisper in my ear how much you love me. I need you to come and meet me where I'm at in a big way. Give me the freedom and the confidence to approach you with all of my needs, in faith. Thank you, Lord. Amen.

Bonus: Ephesians 3:12-20

DAY 28

Psalm 60:11-12

"Give us aid against the enemy, for human help is worthless. With God we will gain the victory, and he will trample down our enemies."

I have some great friends, a great husband, and I go to a great church. I can rely on a number of people to help me out if I need it. But I can't rely on them like I can rely on God. And I can't rely on them to be the sole source of strengthening my faith. No one should be God's stand-in. He alone can bring us true victory—over all of our enemies and in every area of our lives.

Friends, family, and churches all serve a great purpose in our lives. Friends edify us when we need encouragement and commiserate with us when we need comfort. Family members come alongside us and help us carry the load for awhile. Pastors and churches give us a fresh word from God and a place to grow and belong. But the truth is, we can't rely on someone else to do the heavy-lifting when it comes to building up our faith.

God wants to give us the victory, but he also wants to do a lot more that just get us to the end we have in sight. He wants to develop our character, build us up, and show us just how he can come through for us when it seems like all hope is lost. Obviously, that requires some work on our part. We've got to make time for God and reset our priorities.

Do you know the one thing I miss most from my time off while recovering from my work injury? The free hours I had to spend with God. Once I finally got my priorities straight—or more accurately got desperate enough to NEED to put God first—I started making time for God in the mornings. I had two hours to spend with the Lord every morning, and let me tell you, it was glorious. God spoke to me, changed me, and restored me in those times. I was literally hurting and desperate, and I couldn't make it one day without him.

Now I have a demanding part-time job, am writing part-time, and taking care of my injured father. I have to juggle my time to fit in even a few minutes alone with God. When I go a day without time with God I feel lost and out of sync. That's just how much I need him. We need to put him first every day, to seek him every day, and we'll gain the victory. No one said you've got to be perfect, least of all me. Try putting God first today. Then tomorrow. One day at a time. You'll begin to crave your time with him. Let him trample down your enemies.

God, please go before me and prepare the way for me to seek you first. You know my schedule and you know the battles I'm facing. Give me victory and trample down my enemies today. Help me to look to you first, instead of relying on anyone else to give me my word from God. You are my help. With you I will gain the victory. Amen.

Bonus: Read all of Psalm 60 to catch the full meaning of these powerful verses.

DAY 29

Jeremiah 29:11-14a

"For I know the plans I have for you,' declares the Lord, 'plans to prosper you and not to harm you, plans to give you hope and a future. Then you will call upon me and come and pray to me, and I will listen to you. You will seek me and find me when you seek me with all your heart. I will be found by you.'"

Maybe you know this verse by heart. It's one of my favorites. But even for me, it's easy to forget those verses that come after God says he has a plan for me. Yet they are so critical and so vital to God's plan. In fact, they are the key. The verses about calling on him, coming to him, and praying to him are necessary components to drawing closer to God and hearing his voice. His directive to seek him with all our hearts helps us learn to submit and receive grace from him. These parts are crucial to God's plan, for they are the process by which God's plans come about. He's laid it all out right there for us.

Don't miss the promises in this verse. Not only does the Lord declare that he knows exactly the plans he has for us, but he tells us what those plans include. Prosperity, no harm, hope, and a future. Even in the process, God makes promises to us that he will listen to us, and that he will be found by us. All of these are powerful promises that encompass everything we truly need. But finding fulfillment in God isn't always exactly what we want, is it?

I was talking with one of my oldest friends the other day about how our experiences with God in youth group were so drastically different than the way God deals with us today. Back in our teenage exuberance, God gave us clear direction about so many things. Going on missions trips, where to go to school, and our calling to ministry. And now, fifteen years later, it feels like there's just crickets.

Of course, we all want direction. We want to know exactly where we're going. Maybe in our youth we needed God to work like that. But as we grow and develop our faith, God doesn't give us a clear end goal anymore. There's no signpost up ahead saying thirty more miles of rough road. Wouldn't that be nice?

Too many times we seek God just for the plan, but really he's right there with us along the road—where the working of his plan truly is. God's not interested in signposts, end goals, or our definitions of success. He just wants us to learn to cling to him for the whole ride, both in the rough patches and the even ground. How do we do that? By calling on him, coming to him, and praying to him. He wants to listen to us. He wants us to seek him with all our hearts, so we can truly find him as he really is. Always with us.

Lord, thank you for this great reminder of the awesome plans you have for me. Sometimes, even right now, it's hard to believe you will prosper me, give me hope, and a future. But it's right here in your Word. And if you said it, I believe it. Right now I call upon your name. I come before you and pour out my heart. I want to find you right here, in the waiting. Listen to me today as I seek you with all my heart. Amen.

Bonus: Jeremiah 29:10-18

DAY 30

Romans 15:13

"May the God of hope fill you with all joy and peace as you trust in him, so that you may overflow with hope by the power of the Holy Spirit."

As we wrap up thirty days of waiting on the Lord, this beautiful benediction sums up all that we can look forward to simply by trusting in God. These aren't just poetic words. Our God is a God of hope, and he longs to fill us with his joy and peace. All of it. In abundance. We can have his joy and his peace if only we'll learn to trust in him.

Trusting the Lord with our whole life and everything we hope and dream for doesn't come easily. So don't beat yourself up if something pops up tomorrow and you panic first before you even think about trusting God. He made each of us, which also means he knows our nature and our needs. He doesn't expect us to be perfect. He doesn't expect us to blindly trust him without any trace of fear or doubt. If that's what he wanted from us, he would've made robots instead of people.

He just wants us to come to him with everything, including our fears and our doubts. Because he has the antidote—hope, joy, and peace overflowing in us by the power of the Holy Spirit. Sounds amazing, doesn't it? Those are just the byproducts of trusting in him no matter what. Even when we don't understand or can't see a way out, we can still trust him to take care of the mountain in front of us.

Don't you love that last clause? He wants to give us so much hope that it's overflowing—bubbly, vibrant, and contagious. Such overflowing hope comes from the power of the Holy Spirit which is God living in us. That's where the abundance comes from. If we continue to rely solely on ourselves or other people, then we will be stuck with limited resources. The God of hope has more in store for us.

When we start trusting in him and let him work within us, we start to feel his power at work in our hearts and the situations around us. It's hard to let go of our hurts and not try to fix them ourselves. But there are some things we just can't fix on our own. It's painful to admit that. It leaves us feeling powerless and without control. That's because control is an illusion.

If we're not surrendering to God and letting him have control, then we're fighting him for the reins of our own lives. And we won't win that fight. We'll only be wasting our energy and losing ground. I know it's hard. I know it's scary to let go and trust God in everything. But if you're reading this, then I believe you're strong enough to do it. It takes strength and courage to put all our trust in God, but that is the definition of faith.

Believe that he loves you and he knows what he's doing. And you will find all the hope, joy, peace, and power that you could ever need. In abundance.

Lord, I'm so glad that you're the God of hope today. Help me to let go and call up the incredible courage I need to trust in you. I know you are in control, even when I fight you for the reins of my own life. I'm letting go today, laying my life down at your feet. Take control, and help me to keep trusting in you even when things get hard. For I know that you will fill me with all joy and peace by the power of your Holy Spirit. Amen.

Bonus: Romans 15:5-13

CONCLUSION

Dear Reader,

Thank you for joining me on this thirty-day journey of waiting on the Lord. I'm so honored that you took the time to read this book. Believe me, I know the road you're facing is hard. But I also know that God has brought you to this devotional for one purpose—to build you up. I hope that over the last month you've felt God speaking to you and pouring life back into you. He's equipping you for every demanding thing you'll have to face. This is your time to grow closer to God, so keep seeking him no matter what.

Some of the truths in this book come from hard lessons that God taught me in my time of waiting. I wish I could tell you that it all worked out, and that my time of waiting is completely through. But that's not the truth. God has finally fulfilled one big promise he made to me. With this book and the debut of my novel in July, I am a published author. Yet, only by the grace of God. I know he provided the perfect opportunities for me because I waited on him, and he worked everything out in his perfect timing.

Yet, I am still waiting in other areas of my life. Right now, I have no idea what's going to happen with my finances. I just know God's going to come through. And I'm still waiting on his direction for motherhood, which is hard to put on the back burner sometimes. Even still, the Lord has brought me to a place where I can finally trust in him to meet my needs, instead of running around trying to figure things out on my own. I pray that he brings you to that same place.

I've also included a list of my recommended resources—all the books that helped me in the darkest parts of my time spent waiting on the Lord. If you don't find the resources you need, or just want to chat, you can find me on social media or email me at the address below.

Thank you so much for taking the time to read this little offering. You are the reason God laid this book on my heart. I hope God blessed you as you read this book just as much as he blessed me writing it. If you enjoyed this devotional, please leave a review on Amazon. I'd love to hear from you. You can also sign-up for my e-newsletter if you'd like to know about my new releases or book discounts.

Blessings to you,

Barbara Hartzler

Email: barbara.hartzler@gmail.com

Website: www.barbarahartzler.com

AUTHOR BIO

I'm a born-and-raised Missouri native. I live in Kansas City with my wonderful husband and zany dog, Herbie. As a former barista and graphic designer, I love all things sparkly and purple and am always jonesing for a good cup of joe. I earned my Bachelor's degree in Church Communication Arts from Central Bible College with an emphasis on drama and media. In college I won a National Religious Broadcasters/Focus on the Family essay scholarship and wrote and directed a successful one act play.

My first YA novel, *The Nexis Secret*, releases in mid-July 2015 from Splashdown Books. It's inspired by my college experiences and peppered with anecdotes from my New York City missions trip as a teen. Right now, I'm the vice-president of my local ACFW chapter and an active SCBWI member.

I'd love to chat with you or answer any questions you might have. Look for me on the finest social media sites: Twitter, Facebook, Pinterest, Goodreads and my website barbarahartzler.com. Or find me on: Facebook, Twitter:, Goodreads, and Pinterest.

ACKNOWLEDGMENTS

This book has been a blessing to write and an offering that I hope will be just the first fruits of many more books to come. The journey that led me to write this book was a rough road, and I'm profoundly thankful for all the people who've helped and encouraged me along the way. First, thank you to my fabulous husband Sam for his constant love, support, and understanding of the big picture involved in writing this devotional. I'm so grateful to have a champion like you in my corner.

Also, thanks to Lora Young for leading the charge with her own unique journey into indie publishing. Your firstfruits devotional *Abiding: 30 Steps Closer* inspired me to take the Lora Young approach to publishing. To Susan Hollaway, I greatly appreciate your thoughts on this book and am so glad God brought us together for this project. A big thank you to all of my friends of ACFW Kansas City West, Sally Bradley, Donna Geesey, Elizabeth Runyan, Bob Johnson, Heather Manning, Jessica Martin, and Susan Mires. Your support of all my writing endeavors over the years has honed me into the writer I am today.

I'm blessed to have a great family surrounding me. I can't tell you how much I appreciate you for believing in me even in the darkest times when it looked like my publishing dreams were dead. To Bunny and Lloyd Hartzler for always prodding me to write a devotional, and to Whitney Potter, Jr., Christina Potter, and Mary Potter for always believing in me. Knowing you were there to lift me up spurred me to keep trying. Also thank you to my aunts, Marie Davis and Carolyn Dannen, for praying for me and talking me down from the ledge when I needed extra support. A big thank you to my faithful friends, Alle Jones Choate, Sarah Atkinson, Allie Peak, Tena Redenbaugh, and Kelly Irwin who let me vent and were always there to tell me I could do this thing.

Finally, to my Lord and Savior Jesus Christ, for having patience with me and seeing me through the darkest times of my life. I am eternally grateful that I found you, and I'm eternally grateful for the fabulous people who introduced me to you. I am nothing apart from You, God, so thank you for being my strength when I am weak.

RESOURCES

Recommended Books:

L.B. Cowman, *Streams in the Desert* (updated version)

A devotional borne out of a grieving widow's heart. The daily readings in this book make you think about pain, suffering, loss, and waiting on God differently. Some devotions may or may not apply to you, but there's enough solid truth in here to warrant a few readings in your darkest times.

Joni Erickson Tada, *A Place of Healing: Wrestling with the Mysteries of Suffering, Pain, and God's Sovereignty*

A free ebook centered on a quadriplegic's struggle with intense pain and how she finds God and clings to him in the midst of her suffering. An insightful, encouraging read for anyone facing acute or prolong battles with physical pain.

Max Lucado, *Grace for the Moment*

Short excerpts from Max Lucado's greatest works that make for inspirational, thought-provoking, and uplifting daily devotionals. A great 5-minute start to your morning time with God.

Beth Moore, *Believing God*

If you're struggling with fear, doubt, or trust issues, this book is for you. It not only goes into God's promises, but teaches you exactly why you should be believing God will come through for you.

Beth Moore, *Breaking Free* + *Breaking Free Day by Day*

A great set of books for working through any issues still keeping a Christian in bondage such as sin issues, generational issues, and emotional issues. I recommend working through *Breaking Free* first and then following up with the day by day devotional.

Beth Moore, *Praying God's Word + Praying God's Word Day by Day*

This book teaches you how to turn your favorite Bible verses into personal prayers. I highly recommend these books, especially if you start with the book and then dive into the day by day devotional.

Stormie Omartian, *The 7 Day Prayer Warrior Experience*

A short introduction to the power of putting on God's armor and making it personal to your needs.

Lysa TerKuerst, *Craving God: 60 Devotions for Real Women*

This 60-day devotional is for people trying to get healthy, but it's also encouraging in growing closer to God and waiting on him.

Lora Young, *Abiding: 30 Steps Closer*

A simple but profound devotional centered on the life and death of Jesus. A great daily guide to drawing closer to our Savior.

Recommended Songs:

Check out my Waiting on the Lord Playlist on YouTube for 30 days of uplifting and insightful songs to help you in the waiting.